For Rayna –
& Thomas –
it was wonderful
meeting you
both –
talking
with you –

will look
forward to
another time

warmly
Jm

Blue
Tattoo

Blue
Tattoo

Lyn Lifshin

Poems of the Holocaust
Selected and Edited
by Joseph Cowles

Event Horizon Press • 1995

Blue
Tattoo

© 1995 Lyn Lifshin.
All Rights Reserved.

Library of Congress
Catalog Card Number 95-60108
ISBN 1-880391-12-0.

First Printing, May 1995.

Typography and Design
by Joseph Cowles.

Published By:
Event Horizon Press
Post Office Box 867
Desert Hot Springs, CA 92240

Printed and bound in Canada
at Hignell Printing Limited, Winnipeg, Manitoba

Some of these poems
have appeared previously in
or are forthcoming in:

Calyx
Caprice
Jewish Current
Lactuca
Long Shot
New York Quarterly
Painted Bride Quarterly
Response
Slipstream
The William and Mary Review
University of Windsor Review

*For the children
of our children's children
and the generations to follow.*

Foreword

Browsing through a selection of Lyn Lifshin's work awhile back, I came upon three poems that stunned me with their elegant simplicity and raw, wrenching power. In a few lines and with a minimum of words, she captured an essence of the Holocaust experience that has never come through for me in any of the books I've read or films I've seen on the subject.

With an eye toward publishing something to coincide with the 50th anniversary of Victory in Europe Day, my immediate (and rather naïve) response was to write and ask Lyn if she might have available any other work on this subject. A few days later the mail brought a large, heavy envelope. Inside were hundreds of poems—a treasure trove!

The preceding year the New York State Museum had asked Lyn to put together a workshop, *Writing Through The Holocaust* as part of a lecture exhibit. "Although I had written poems about the Holocaust before," Lyn told me, "to prepare for this workshop I submerged myself in films, writing, everything I could which dealt with that time. As a result, I ended up writing almost exclusively about the Holocaust for an extended time."

And write she did. That initial package and the various smaller missives Lyn sent during the following months generated approximately 600 poems from which to choose and edit the nearly 200 that comprise Blue Tattoo.

Although rooted in countless centuries of racial hatred, the events specific to the Holocaust escalated rapidly within the span of a few years. This collection of poems is arranged in a sequence somewhat parallel to that in which the events transpired. This arrangement is rather loose, because similar things took place at different times in different locations.

Each poem was originally written as an individual work meant to stand alone. Through the selection and editing process they have been brought together as a unit.

Blue Tattoo begins with the rise to power of Adolf Hitler and the National Socialist German Workers' (Nazi) Party in the mid Thirties, and the anti-Semitic hostilities that escalated into Kristallnacht ("the night of broken glass") in November 1938—ultimately resulting in the massacre of six million Jews during World War II.

Lyn's poetry recalls the ghetto experience, selection and deportation to the concentration camps, the inhumanity and terrors of the camps, and the exterminations. Her poems on the liberation reflect the experiences of the liberators as well as those being liberated. The final poems deal with memories of the Holocaust, and an attempt to resolve those memories.

While not intended to provide a history of the Holocaust, it is hoped that the poems in *Blue Tattoo* will enable the reader to gain a powerful, intimate experience of the people and events. Great poetry does that. With a few well-chosen words, a skilled poet can tap into the three-dimensional, multi-sensory wide screen theatres of our minds, projecting scenes that bring forth every emotion. And Lyn Lifshin's skills are *prime!*

Some of these poems treat similar subject matter from only slightly different perspectives, causing the sharp edge of the test to become blunted. This is intentional. The Nazi dehumanization process was designed to kill the spirit long before the body was destroyed. If you find yourself becoming numb to the horrors, you can set the book aside for awhile, go for a walk, get away from it. In the late Thirties there was no way for one to get away, and the world looked on (often closing apathetic eyes) to what was happening.

At a luncheon several years ago, someone I thought I knew rather well said to me, with complete sincerity, "You know, there never really was a Holocaust. Those were Depression times all over the world, and the Jews, well, they were at the bottom of the totem pole, so they got less of what little food was available. There was no planned extermination; they simply starved to death."

One would think a well-educated person would know better. But you know: the eyewitnesses—those survivors who can tell the stories first hand—are few, and will soon have passed on altogether. While it doesn't seem possible that the truth of the Holocaust atrocities could ever be seriously doubted, or that some form of Nazism—some form of "ethnic cleansing"—could ever gain a new foothold, perhaps this glance back at the events of a half-century ago will remind us that we are wise to keep a close watch on conditions in our own era.

—JRC

Diary Entry
Lodz Ghetto

These pages
that I now begin to write
would lead to certain death
if ever they were found.
But what is death?
How few
of those I knew here
are still alive today,
how close to death
we all stand.
I can die here any moment
even if I take
the gravest care.
Why should I not
endeavor,
even in the midst
of these conditions,
to tell this gruesome story
that no longer
gives goose flesh?

Germany
The Thirties

Brown uniforms.
Arms raised up.
The swastika.
The cheering crowd.
Hitler behind roses.
A wave of people
yelling *Heil Heil.*
Leaves are flattened
under black cars,
smoke rises from
books burning.

For Me The Holocaust
Started In '33
In A Small Village

I was in a class
and the teacher said
I hear we have
a Jew pig in this class.
I shook. He said
I'm going to show
this Jew pig
how much pain
a Jew can survive.
He took a stick
out of the desk
and hit and hit.
I don't remember the pain,
but only the kids
who'd once been my friends
laughing and laughing.

Photograph
In A Newspaper

A Jewish Family
in some German town,
an ordinary family
snapped mid-passage
down a cobbled street:
the father in glasses,
short in a lumpy topcoat,
felt hat;
the mother plump,
two scrawny kids in leggings
carrying a school bag.
Maybe they were trying
to herd the children
to school to keep them
from being beaten.
Here they seem frozen,
as if arrested
by a curse, a taunt,
an obscenity—
trapped in leafy trees,
trim stores,
three storm troopers
in military uniforms,
six or seven years
before the furnaces.

Sounds Of Glass

The woman
who cannot see
hears what sounds like
branches slapping

into a frozen lake,
sounds like glass
under her husband's
foot at the wedding—
musical as wind chimes.
She rolls in a bed
that grew too big,
pulls
the feather down quilt
closer.
It was blue once,
the blue of an
August sky,
when the beads he brought
twisted each other,
sounded like icy water,
caught light like diamond.
Light she can't see,
a new blackness
she can't see.

Father Told Me
We Couldn't Go
To A Certain Bank

Why? *I asked.*
It's closed to Jews.
But we're not Jews, *I said.*
Yes, we are.
That night was
Kristallnacht.
My father avoided
being captured by
riding the streetcar
all night.

We rode by a
synagogue on fire,
its windows smashed.
My father grabbed a
mosaic tile, said to me:
Keep it. Remember.

Kristallnacht

Someone
who knows the words
for *glass* and *break*
only in German,
in a house only other
well-to-do Germans visit,
Germans who've
lived in Germany
as long as they can trace.
There is no Menorah.
No one lights
candles on Fridays.
All the daughters
have long blonde braids.
The songs are of *Noël.*
One son is named Noel.
Then the night
starts to sound like
those crystal stars falling
onto the marble;
a whole house
of stars crashing
as Dresden
is bombed
with stars getting
closer.

Torah

The huge dome
of stained glass—
cherry, lime, guava
and raspberry—
shatters,
a snow of glass ankle deep
in jagged pieces.
Then they throw
the Torah in the air,
saying,
Wipe your asses with it!

After Kristallnacht

Yanking off a boy's clothes
to see if he is circumcised,
they rip the cotton away.
The father wants
to keep his underwear on
but they won't let him:
they tear off his clothes
and shoot him.
Corpses are coated with
urine, shit, sweat,
and menstrual blood.
Children's bodies fly
through the air.
With hooks
they pry mouths open,
with pliers and hammers
break jaws apart,
to look for
gold teeth.

Warsaw
September 1939

Streets without lights,
the railroad station transformed.
No people with magazines
and sweets, at the canteen
laughing and chatting—
but dark, deserted.
Police with guns
demand identification.
Only fifty or so
on the train
that moves so slowly,
the tracks bombed, torn.
Planes moving in:
explosions,
then screams.
A woman shocked
to see a man's hand
severed,
hanging from his wrist
by a small piece of skin,
his good one holding
his torn bleeding hand.

Poland
September 1939

After the train is bombed,
children who've left school
walk along the tracks,
walk and hitch for days
to the outskirts of Lubla,
through bomb craters—

hear air raid sirens,
see Polish soldiers
with machine guns
on roofs of the buildings,
whole blocks on fire,
only a bomb crater to hide in,
tall buildings crashing,
low flying planes,
bricks, glass and rubble
spitting, crashing,
hundreds killed
in a few minutes,
smoke blackening the sun.

When The Borders Close

People stow away,
slip through
black water
at night.
It is like a hike
through black leaves,
everyone together
in a clump.
My parents had a
three year old baby girl.
Everyone was taking hold,
caring for each other.
Wet birch and maples.
Whispering
under a blood moon.
Then Germans
ambush
as the boat pulls out:
the child

held by her blonde hair—
a sneering tall Gestapo,
his knife against
her wet face.

Color Of Law

Blue.
Blue of tattoos,
of crusty blood.
The law has no color
of anything growing.
Not green, an earth color.
Not what is natural.
Color of law is blue,
a gas of Zyklon B.
Blue of what changes skin,
indelible bruise blue
of tortured rose
smelled and buried.

The First Atrocities

SS men rip
clumps of hair
from Jews' beards
and sometimes
set their heads on fire.
Routinely,
Jewish women and girls
are raped in the squares.
In an occupied town
in the Ukraine
a mob of Gentiles

ties a Jewish woman's hair
to the tail of a horse
and drives the animal off.
The horse drags the woman
until her whole face
is completely disfigured
and there isn't
a sign of life
from her body.
Most of the crowd
is hysterical
with laughter.

Terezin

As crimes grow
more bestial
the façade is
brightened up:
no more newspaper
prints of nude women
wailing to death on
the heaps of dead,
no press handouts,
no syndicated halftones
or newsreel clips
about murder camps,
the blood and smoke hidden.
They plant
trees and flowers.
People are starved
and dying of typhus,
though at night
they have American jazz
from the café.

Faces In Kiev

Jovial fat men at the beach
in undershirt bathing suits.
A brother and sister
giggling in snow with skis
near a young girl
in a white dress.
With a serious stare
another pedals
a large bicycle.
Six children in
winter coats and hats
try not to laugh.
A family boats on a still,
sun-dappled river.
Children in swings,
grown-ups in hammocks.
Young lovers
on paths of roses,
babies in their arms.
Five burly woodcutters
and a young girl
with gypsy eyes.
Two teenagers strike a pose
of bohemian daring—
she's in boots and a visor cap,
bending as he lights
her cigarette.
A tiny boy in a sailor suit
perches on a chair.
A half century of images
from one town where,
after 900 years,
Nazis machine-gun everyone
in two days.

As Bread Is
Being Distributed

In the dark air
far from the windows
one can hear the band
beginning to play.
The healthy comrades
are leaving in squads for work.
The tunes are few,
a dozen,
the same ones
every morning and night.
They lie engraved
on our minds,
will be the last thing
we shall forget,
the perceptible expression
of geometrical madness,
of the resolution
of others
to annihilate us
first as men
in order to kill us
more slowly afterward.

Ghetto Nights,
Deep Summer August

After 9 p.m.,
after fifteen hours
of exhausting work,
men and women
race from the bedbugs,
look for a spot they can

rest their swollen legs.
Deformed legs shuffle along,
dry shrunken lungs
breathe heavily.
Bodies fall on wet boards.
They slip off sandals,
tell of dreams of supplements,
fantasize about a food ration.
Some who get there late
have no room, stand around,
see a wagon in the sky.
One man tells a story
of the Messiah—
When the Messiah comes,
we'll cook potatoes
with young onions
and we'll spare no butter—
other fantasies are woven
until it is time for a nap,
maybe dreams
that will take them back
to those lands of fantasy.
Before they leave,
the bodies line up at the walls
as in mysterious ritual,
relieve themselves
of all the water
they've guzzled during the day,
soups, cabbage, vegetables.
Puddles form in the night
and their stench bears witness
to stomachs ruined
on the ghetto diet,
bodies ruined but stubborn,
that seem sworn
to not give in.

Near The Water Closet

Heine's poems
and Hebrew scripture
for toilet paper.
A fight over cheese.
After the uproar,
talk of family.
A son somewhere,
wife somewhere else,
daughter—
who knows where?
What do they get to eat?
In New York,
someone says, *you can*
get a gigantic sandwich
for a nickel:
sardines,
sauerkraut,
cheese on white bread
with olives.
Stop it! another cries.
Such talk is dangerous.

Supply And Demand

One eats what is available
when it's available
and how much is available.
Dirty turnips, last year's
carrots, stinky fish.
All the Germans allow
to be sold. One sells
something for something
until there is nothing.

When The Potatoes Come

Everyone is smiling,
praising God, cuddling
the potatoes—potatoes
like apples and figs,
not black, not rotting.
Women weigh them
on a scale, then rub
the potatoes to their skin.
Potatoes! In the middle
of dying, in a house where
five have died in a year.
Potatoes from God!
weeps a woman who has
just buried her children
in stranger's shrouds.

Ghetto Salad

Stinks.
It's the potatoes, the peelings,
grade B partly rotten
beet leaves
not left to die a natural death,
but making a detour
through the ghetto's intestines.
Dark leaves soaked in barrels,
dried in sun,
splashed with bread,
sautéed in a pan
with real butter and caraway,
paprika, salt—any spice,
to just tame the salad's
ghetto aroma.

Starvation

In the hospital a man yells
Papa, Mama,
give me a piece of bread!
Another who can't sleep
loses his temper, yells
If you don't keep quiet
I'll come and throw you
into the yard!
Next morning
the man is dead
and the sleepless
one is ashamed, sorry.

Young Girl's Diary

There is nothing to eat.
We are going to die of hunger.
My teeth ache,
my left leg is frostbitten.
I almost finished the honey.
What have I done?
How selfish I am!
What are they going to say?
What will they
spread on their bread now?
Mother looks terrible—
a shadow of herself.
She works very hard.
Whenever I wake up
at twelve or one in the night
she is bent
over the sewing machine,
and she gets up at six.

I have no heart, no pity,
eat everything
I can lay my hands on.
Today I had an argument
with Father.
I insulted and even cursed him.
And this was because yesterday
I weighed the noodles
but this morning took
a spoonful for myself.
When Father came back
he weighed them,
found there was less,
started yelling at me.
He was right, but I was
upset and cursed him.
Father just stood
at the window
and cried like a child.
No stranger
ever abused him like I did.
Everybody was home.
I went to bed quickly.
I thought I would die of hunger.

Yellow Stars

An elderly woman
sells arm bands—
some of paper
some of linen.
She does well.
If you have
a crumpled or dirty one
the Germans beat you.

Scraps

From the Germans
they learn the value
of scraps.
Even rags will be turned
again and again,
put to use.
A towel will be a washcloth;
a shredded dress a diaper,
a bandage for a finger
so small it won't take much.

In The Ruins
Of A Brick Factory

In the mounds of waste
and puddles of mud
where maids used to
throw away coal and
coal dust with the garbage,
hundreds of people dig,
their backs bent crooked,
using bent iron hooks,
spades, shovels,
scraping for anything
to bring warmth.

In One House
In The Ghetto

Seventeen people
in three beds,
the old woman
whose house it is
pushed to a back corner
of the room, paralyzed,
without even a mattress.
For the infant
of the daughter-in-law
who died,
eighteen months old,
not even rations.
He calls all the others
Daddy or *Mama*
but like the old woman
he has no one.

Evening Visit

One night
two German cars
move slowly
along the street.
SS men go into
an apartment
across the way.
A light goes on
in a window
of the first floor.
Moments later
they come out
with a man
wearing only
pajama pants.
They stand him
up against the wall
and step back
to take a photograph,

positioning the subject.
The man
raises one hand
to shield his face.
A burst of bullets
and he slides down.

The Dancer

When I was thirteen
I was ordered
to do a Hasidic dance
around a heap
of naked corpses
for two crumbs of bread.
You think it's not easy
to become a street walker
when you're starving?
I'd lost 46 pounds.
Still, we had to bow
and salute every Nazi,
take off our hats,
or we'd be toothless
and eyeless.

Selling Themselves
In The Ghetto

People who have
either nothing to lose
or who are reckless
or desperate,
believing they are drawing
accurate conclusions

about the general situation,
volunteer as substitutes.
They sell themselves.
A human being is worth
three loaves of bread,
a half kilogram of margarine,
one pound of sugar,
plus, perhaps, shoes
and other items of clothes.

Exception To The Rule

There were
some Germans
who were different.
One ran to my
neighbor's wife,
asked if she
was a Jewess,
gave her
a loaf of bread.

In The Thick Hot Smelly
September Heat

General curfew
from 5 p.m. until
further notice.
Those not complying
will be evacuated.
Food stores are empty,
street peddlers selling
food have disappeared.
People who believe in God

toy with suicide.
The human brain
cannot comprehend it.
Anyone surviving this
will lose all memory of it,
will not believe it
himself.

German Document
Sent To
The Eldest Of Jews

Regarding machines
in the ghetto:
We request that you
immediately investigate
whether there is
a bone grinder
in the ghetto,
either with a motor
or hand driven.
The special command
in Chelmno
is interested in such a grinder.

Short Supply

From some windows
all one can see
is an undertaker's shop.
One day, without
enough men to round up,
they take the undertaker,
leave the corpse.

In Passing

Every day someone dies.
Sometimes three or seven.
No one notices corpses.
A pretty girl shows
displeasure
when someone carrying a corpse
disturbs her
as she moves lipstick
across her face.

Detachment

There is
a marked indifference
to death.
One walks past corpses;
few go to the hospital
to visit a relative,
or to the grave yard.
150 die a day.
The death rate grows,
they bury at night.
There's a shortage
of burial grounds.
Several
in one coffin
all buried
at the same time
with one mad man
running after the departed
screaming,
Did he leave
his bread card?

The Lost

Stench.
Naked corpses on the street.
There isn't money
for burial taxes.
People strip the clothes;
every ring counts.
Men and women
stand there, not living,
not yet dead.
Someone with three onions,
someone with a cookie.
Not like human beings.
Someone, mouth open,
as if to speak,
if he could, of what
you wouldn't believe.

An Opportunity

There was nothing
in the streets
but the dead.
Heaps of corpses.
We had to step over them.
There wasn't room to work.
Besides fighting the Germans
we fought starvation
and thirst.
We had no contact
with the world.
We were cut off.
We could no longer
understand why

we were fighting.
We thought of
trying a break out
to get to the Aryan side.
We found a tunnel.
Early in the morning
we suddenly emerged
in a street in bright daylight,
May 1, a sunny day,
stunned to find ourselves
among normal people
as if we'd come from
another planet.
People jumped on us
because we looked
so exhausted.
Skin in rags.
Around the ghetto
there were always
suspicious Poles
who grabbed Jews.
By a miracle, we escaped.

Lodz Diary

Am without a place to live,
am without bread,
without potatoes.
Have never been
so forsaken.
My daughter,
what is she thinking?
Does she know, poor thing?
Is she thinking of the
28th of November 1937,

of our chicken and poppy torte?
My golden child.
Will I see her again?

German Document

The Registrar office
is complaining that
in recent death notices
the cause of death
has been given as
hunger, starvation,
a swelling from hunger.
Such references have to stop.
The general term
malnutrition
must be used instead.

Hearsay

It is rumored
that there is a plan
to establish a summary court
that will give
death sentences
for political crimes:
radio listening,
spreading "false information,"
and even for political beliefs.
The ghetto, of course,
immediately shuts up
and there is no political gossip.
A miraculous remedy,
this rumor.

Inside The Church In Lodz

It is all feathers,
a thick layer of white.
Waves of feathers
rise into the air
with each step,
each movement.
Every breeze blows up
a cloud of feathers.
The altar of carved wood,
figures of saints,
the huge organ,
covered with feathers
that undulate in the breeze.
And in the middle,
men and women
wrapped in white,
sitting, running, standing.
White figures in the
dark stained light.
A small sign
attached to the entrance
reads
Institute for Feather Cleaning
but not that it is in this
Church of the Virgin Mary
where bedding is brought,
robbed from Jews
who are sent from Lodz
and murdered.
There in gold
and blood light,
pillows and featherbeds
are ripped open,

the feathers cleaned,
sorted, packed
and shipped to Germany
to merchants
who sell them to
support the Reich.

Lodz Diary
Friday, February 28

The weather cloudy,
8 degrees.
14 arrests for theft,
15 for other crimes.
45 died today in the ghetto.
No births were registered.

Overcrowding

You can't die either,
these days,
complains a woman
who has to arrange
formalities
in the mortuary office
in connection with
her mother's death.
With the increase
in the death rate
there is a minimum
of three days wait
to bury the dead.
Then there aren't
enough horses left

to draw the hearses.
Some days a sideless
hauling wagon
has to be used
piled with
several dozen bodies
at one time.

Homeward Bound

There's a minimum
of three days wait
to bury the dead
and sometimes ten days.
Even with 200 grave diggers
only 50 graves
can be dug
in the hard ground.
Hearse driver,
who are you going
to pick up?
I'll find someone—
we have enough corpses.
And who will pick you up?
No one will have to.
My mare will bring me
to the cemetery.
She knows the way.

A Small Example

At 6 p.m.
all members of Lodz
are told to be

at Fischplatz at 9 p.m.
20,000 stand in the cold,
see a just put up gallows.
Some women faint,
others start to weep.
A low dais,
three steps up,
a rectangular trap door.
Well-fed SS in field grey.
Soldiers with machine guns.
Silence. Shivering.
The soldiers in overcoats.
The victim shivers.
They take his topcoat.
He climbs to the platform.
Please let me live,
I have broken no laws.
He glances away.
A dull thumping of
something heavy on wood,
and a second later
a twitching body
jerks in the air.

A Young Girl's Diary Lodz Ghetto

Saturday, 7 March.
Beautiful sunny day today.
When the sun shines,
my mood is lighter.
How sad life is.
One yearns for something
better than this gray.
When we look at

the fences that separate us
from the rest of the world,
our souls like birds in a cage
yearn to be free.
How I envy the birds.
Longing breaks my heart
and I wonder if
I will ever live in better times.
After the war
will I be with my parents
and friends? Will I live
to eat bread and rye flour
until I am full?

What The Police Find

Mucky paths
half covered with snow.
Scruffy children,
faces wrinkled.
Yellow dirty snow.
A wagon with people
harnessed to it.
When police go into
apartments to yank
the deportees away
they find starved
children, old people
frozen to death, bark
stripped from trees,
mice frozen
in the middle of rooms
next to shoes and rags
they had not been
too weak to bite apart.

Release

Prisoners commit suicide
on the electrified
barbed wire,
hands clenched
in a death grip.
Suspended by their wrists,
two tortured inmates
dangle from trees,
buxom women
flayed until
their breasts are in ribbons,
then hung upside down
for the dogs to finish.

The Last Days Of Lodz

A German official
notices a doctor's
beautiful
16 year old daughter,
grabs her in the hallway,
drags her into his office,
tries to rape her,
and when she screams
shoots her in the eye.

Hiding Out The Last Night
In Lodz Ghetto

*We sit on top of a suitcase
we brought to the dungeon.
We have a supply of water,*

*about 600 liters,
and we decided that
each of us will get
three glasses of water
per day.
We've pooled
all the fat we had—
oil, butter and margarine.
In the morning we
distribute our rations.
Our nervousness
exceeds the limits
of human endurance.
We think constantly
that the Germans
will come into the courtyard
looking for us.
Water drips from
the dungeon walls.
There's a lack of oxygen,
a lighted match
goes out fast.
We've heard the Germans
are to transport us
to the Jewish cemetery
where a week ago
they ordered nine large
graves to be dug—
each for a hundred people.
Any minute now
the search will begin.
If they find our hiding place,
I will leave these notebooks
in the dungeon.
They might be
our last trace.*

Leaving Warsaw

It wasn't hard to pack.
Not much to choose from:
two pair of pants,
a sweater.
The only valuable possession,
high riding boots
from my father,
with new soles.
The immediate problem:
to outlast the boots.

Before Departure

People look for light,
easy to carry bags.
The blind, the lame,
the dying
are yanked out of hospitals.
Some throw themselves
into cleaning,
choosing things.
Heads are shaved;
they look like prisoners;
give up house keys,
personal documents,
money and gold;
sign forms
they are not
allowed to read
the contents of;
are no longer
people but
deportees.

I Sold My Jewelry

Bought salami and cookies.
My mother told me this,
but not how the police
came to arrest her first,
asked,
Where are your children?
We won't harm them.
You'll be reunited and
relocated.
They smiled, took her
to the central stadium.
Other Jews waited
with shapeless bundles,
the last shreds of who they were
before the flamenco
of black boots
ground even that
under their staccato.

Emptying The Hospitals

Relatives with swollen feet
run from all corners
of the ghetto.
Forget soup, forget potatoes.
Roads are blocked.
Fathers, wives, husbands,
mothers stand wringing
their hands, their throats
letting go with crude
nonhuman sobs.
The bedridden and sick
are thrown on the road

like calves driven
to slaughter.
The sick who can run
jump from upper stories,
hide in cellars,
impersonate attendants.
Many who keep calm live.

Deportation Summons

Wedding invitations
they call them.
800 people a day
have to be supplied.
When they go into
the apartments
of those deported
they find starved children,
babies frozen to flannel.

Rybna Street

The police have to
take people out of their
apartments. There they
encounter resistance,
rip babies from their
mother's breasts,
drag out grown children,
tear husband from wife,
people who have lived
together 40 years or 50.
The police surround a house,
block entrances,

chase the people
like mice into traps.

Removal

Stormy night;
daybreak is cool.
Police surround houses,
screaming. Women appear.
*Girls, old women
up into the wagon.*
Children thrown like
packages. In front,
a German officer with whip,
soldiers with rifles,
revolvers, steel helmets.
Widows must be shot.
Faces press to glass.

Nightmare

Mothers
run through the streets,
only one shoe on,
hair barely combed,
shawls dragging.
They still keep children
at their sides, clasp them
even more tightly
to emaciated breasts,
still pour kisses
onto the little faces.
The eyes don't know
about tomorrow.

At Number 7
Zytnia Street

The widow of a doctor
who tried to escape Dachau
and was shot, is taken
from her apartment
into the courtyard
for selection, holding
her small child, four,
a blonde with lake eyes.
They smile to one another,
the child happy that
Mother has taken her
out to the yard
in warm August light.
The mother smiles, too—
to show courage, health,
that she is capable
of working. The soldier,
a good party man,
knows the baby must be taken.
She won't, no, give away
the child, she says, as long
as she lives; smiles on.
He doesn't believe
she will resist,
keep resisting.
He is well bred—
a Prussian military school—
knows to be polite to women
(doesn't know if this
means Jewish women too).
Neighbors look,
are quietly weeping.
The mother and daughter

still smile.
The soldier gives them
three minutes together, asks,
Well, how is it?
What did you decide?
She has nothing to decide,
nothing has changed,
not even the smile.
His gets darker.
Turn to the wall!
She turns with the same smile,
holds the child's hand
more convulsively
so the child turns her head
slightly to the mother.
It is as if their fingers hold
a secret
as he squeezes the trigger.

Memory Is Not Only
A Spring, But A Tomb

Mother still thinks of
how she scowled—scowled
and threw a tantrum.
Everything was normal,
then, in a day,
they were spitting on us.
The Germans said
Ten minutes to pack what
you need. Mother sat,
kicked against the
piano stool, said she
wouldn't leave her Steinway.
She was just learning

to play Strauss,
her long blonde hair
and blue eyes
lighter than those
of the Austrian ladies
waltzing on the cover
of the piano book.
And though her mother's
face went white,
she would not stop
kicking.

Children's Transport

Blimele,
with her blonde curls,
blue eyes, her
Yiddish writer-father's muse,
is grabbed while
her mother,
a month early,
delivers a new baby sister
(the fears of the children's
roundup shoved her
early into the light,
a dot with two fists,
still with no name).
The mother
weak and trembling
lies in postpartum fever,
the father chasing
ghetto flies
from her face.
He can't tell her
the other daughter's gone.

Only the infant screams,
half dead.
The mother becomes weaker,
more feverish.
The father
can't show what he feels,
tries to console her
with words that
chill him
with their lie.
Blimele will be okay.
Jewish police will
hold on to the child
of a Jewish writer.
He tries
to convince his wife
that he couldn't say this
calmly
if it weren't true—
as she gets weaker,
lies in a half dream,
doesn't see his body
drenched in sweat,
the trapped tears
leaking through his skin.

Irena's Story

All week, distant barking
of dogs, guns, shouts
in German: Alle Juden raus!
All Jews out. Thousands
of people brought on wagon
to the hospital, taken
in trucks to the unknown.

The last day of deportations
we get up at six a.m., drink
boiled water with saccharine.
Luckily, our street has
already been gone through.
But suddenly, gunshots!
Orders are shouted for
all Jews to come out.
Rifle butts bang the door,
Mother grabs my arm—
Maybe we can hide.
Father tries to calm us:
Rub your cheeks,
bite your lips, straighten up
and walk with a smile.
Father is 56 but looks fine.
His face swollen with hunger
looks round and full.
His well-rubbed cheeks,
normal color; no grey hairs.
Mother is thin, her face drawn,
her hair white.
But she is only 42
and her shy eyes
have a beautiful young smile.
We move slowly
through selection.
I am told to go to the right.
I wait, feel my body
a petrified bundle
of muscles and nerves.
Others come,
but not my parents.
I elbow my way through
the crowd of people,
start running

toward the Germans,
see a hand raised,
recognize a neighbor's face.
When I reopen my eyes
I'm standing near the same
people who tried to hide me.
When I get home
I see a classmate, Fryda,
on the stairway, like a mute,
her parents also
never returned.

After The Curfew,
After The Selection

People who are safe,
who come out of hiding,
feel like they are newly born.

After The Selection

Old people who had
hidden themselves
come back weak—
some haven't eaten for days—
held by relatives
so they don't fall over.
In the courtyard
a woman bewails,
What do I have in life?
My twelve year old boy
shot today,
my girls six and fourteen
taken away.

The Greeting

Thousands
stand in front of stores
to get rations
after seven days of hunger.
People greet one another,
wish each other well
for the New Year,
like after an earthquake
or shipwreck.
Did you get through?
Who was taken?
My brother. My mother.
My parents. My children.

Other Side Of The Fence

People freeze to death
at a train station
where they have to wait
seven hours to depart.
The price of bread
soars beyond the reach
of almost everyone.
It can't be worse there.
I'd gladly eat from
a pig's trough if only
to get out of this ghetto.

Left Behind

After the evacuation
the closest relatives

of evacuees
dive into their bread,
sometimes without tears.
There is a terrible
hardening and brutalizing
of the spirit.
Best friends feel no pain.
People do not answer
questions.

Why The Charcoal
In Grainy
World War II Movies
Always Seems
More Blue Than Black

Because the trains
are always departing.
Because *I* could have been
in the clang of rails,
maybe in a cattle car.
Blue of smashed delft,
of the stained glass,
clattering.
Somewhere,
an aunt I might
have been named for,
some Raisal, a rose,
crammed into a car
so packed no one can
squat to pee,
focuses on a sliver of sky,
goes over all the Dvořak
violin sonatas in her head
to not go crazy,

holds the blue in
until it leaks out on her arm,
those tattooed numbers.

Freight

They are so exhausted
few can do little but
fool themselves about
the transport.
*These are freight cars
but you will be switched
on the way.*
Ten hours after they depart
trains come back empty.
A note in one wagon says
*The deportees are
approaching Chelmno,
a slaughterhouse.*
Someone writes in a diary,
*If a ghetto man
got power over the world
he would destroy it—
and he would be doing
the right thing.*

The Trains

Farmers work fields,
hear the screams.
At first it is unbearable.
You get used to anything.
The Jews wait, weep,
ask for water,

die naked in the cars.
Some Poles
do give them water.
It is dangerous.
When a woman
asks for water
a guard shoots her.
Blood and brains all over.
One survivor will say
*They laughed at the train,
took joy,
gave no water.*

Arrival

Some have been traveling
fourteen to sixteen days,
are half crazy, starved.
The children beg for water.
Please, water.
Nothing to drink for days.
They are dying of thirst.
They are already being
exterminated.
When the SS say *Undress,
undress and there'll be tea,*
they are so parched they rush
into the gas chamber.

He Says They Are
Going To Heidebreck

As soon as the people
get out of the vans

they are blinded by
spotlights, herded
down a corridor to
the *Undressing Room,*
beaten, made to run,
bloodied. Those who
can't run fast enough
are beaten to death.
In the room, they know.
They've heard the rumors.
They panic.
Children cling to each other,
to their mothers.
The old cry.
An SS officer enters.
He gives his word
that they'll be transferred
to Heidebreck.
They cry out!
A trick! We were lied to!
We want to live, to work!
The officer stares at them.
Guards surge forth
with clubs, trying to
force the people to undress.
Most refuse, begin singing
the Czech anthem and Hativah.

Something New To Learn

They are on the train
for several days.
It is winter
but they heat it up
with their bodies.

Suddenly the train stops.
The doors open.
SS with dogs are all around.
There are lights in the sky.
They get off,
are made to line up.
There are people with
striped uniforms.
Someone asks, in Czech,
Where are we?
Someone understands,
says *Auschwitz.*
They don't yet know
what the word means.

Incredulous

They are led into a family camp.
Children, men, women,
together for the selection.
Men come in, tell them
Auschwitz is where
they are burning people.
They don't believe it.
In the camp
there is a transport
that had left before them.
All that is left: some shoes.
They hadn't believed it either.

Auschwitz

There is an electrical fence.
You can't climb it

but can speak through it.
Families are taken together.
They take their luggage
into the camp.
Their hair isn't cut.
They are treated differently
than anyone here has seen.
These people have
special cards that say
gassing and quarantine.
They're to be kept six months.
There is a school for their
children, a theatre.
They are told to write letters
to relatives in the ghetto
to say they are working,
together.
The SS take the children
to play at Heidi Branch.
At midnight the parents
receive a note.
The *Lake of Ashes* is where
the cremated are dumped.
There is no Heidi;
the train runs right to
the crematorium.

Letter From Nazi Transit Camp

*I can not get over this
incredibly beautiful spring.
I go to the clinic three times
a week for heat treatment
for my arm which was*

*starting to bother me again.
However, there is always
a long line of children
with rickets waiting,
and I would not want to
take the place of any of them.
I would like to ask you
to send my blue spring coat.
I believe I can finally let go
of a green winter one.
Please have it "decorated" first.
Did you receive my last
shipment of dirty laundry?
I apologize for the messy
packing but it had to be done
in a terrible hurry and the
towels hadn't even been
dried yet after my shower.
I was sorry to see my good
wool stockings had faded
so much. In this week
I had the great misfortune
to break two combs in a row
and would be much obliged
if you could dig up another
of those instruments for me,
preferably a very coarse one.
I would also like a bit of
brilliantine. I seem to
remember there was a bottle
with some left in it
near the bathroom sink.
I do have to rave about the
tomato juice although not as
much fun as sitting around
our faithful black stove.*

It was quite good anyway
and very agreeable.
Much relieved that D. was
not on yesterday's transport.
I was awfully pleased with
the lovely bar of Maya soap
you included. Should I start
trying to get a suitcase sent
in this direction? And if so,
which one? Probably my
good leather accordion
suitcase would be the best.
It's tough and otherwise
I might not get to use it
for awhile. If I should have
to leave it behind soon,
I might have to do without it
the rest of my days.

Letter From
Alice Jacquelin Luzghart
To Her Mother

Dear Mommy,
Thank you for the clogs.
My feet will be warm now.
The snow is melting
and the sun is out.
Soon it will be spring
with trees blossoming
and budding.
I hope you got my letter
asking you to take pictures.
I forget what the south
looks like. Of course

I was very small
when I lived there.
Fay is going to send me
the blue checked skirt.
I have nothing else to say
so I'll stop here and
send you a big kiss.
Your loving daughter,
Jacquelin.

Prisoner's Letter
To His Wife

I would never have believed
that I could one day
be so miserable, and yet
all this suffering would be
bearable if I knew that
it is not for nothing,
that I'll get out in the end.
Our last vacation trip
was so beautiful,
so harmonious.
The sketches from that trip,
they are my last and best.
They have to be kept safe.

Letter One
From Camp Westerbrook

Please don't complain
that you have to spend
so much time traveling.
Don't forget that at least

you are doing it
of your own volition.
We've had a few weeks respite
at a price though;
very serious illnesses
such as diptheria, hepatitis,
thirty cases of polio.
But in spite of this
another transport
scheduled for Tuesday.
You may begin to understand
that under the circumstances
we do not consider
the loss of a wrist watch
a disaster.
Keep in mind,
we had to leave our homes
at a moment's notice,
were allowed to take only
what we could carry.
Not only did we lose
furniture and other valuables
which will certainly
be impossible to replace
in the first few years,
but all the memories
attached to them.
The worst thing for me
was when I returned home
the third time, I forgot
to take an enamel dish
and a little cooking pot.
My mother-in-law forgot
her back pack with
warm clothes and underwear.
So stop grieving for your

wrist watch. I shall be
happy to buy you one
if only one tenth of the rest
will turn out all right.
First let us hope we'll be
reunited in good health
and freedom.
In the meantime,
it is beginning to look
as if we'll first have to make
a little detour . . .

Letter Two
From Camp Westerbrook

I am sorry there is
no chance of matzohs
but I suppose we will
survive without them too.
I for one won't shed
a tear about it.
On the other hand,
I would like another
loaf of black rye
if it is not too hard to get.
The round bread with
poppy seed looks delicious
but I haven't cut it yet.
I think I will take that
tomorrow when I go
for supper.
Those little challa loaves
were wonderful too,
and just today I ate
the last piece of the lot

you sent me about
two weeks ago.
They do not get stale,
and keep their flavor
to the last crumb.

Bundles Start Coming

Improvised sacks
packed by someone
not the owner:
clothes, papers, bedding,
ID cards. No one knows
where they come from.
800 tons of clothes,
35 tons of shoes,
passed through
deinfestation gates
(jackets and coats ripped
along the seams),
prayer shawls.
Papers drawn up in the ghetto.
Items of clothing some
recognize from someone
who has gone.

Summer Event

1,300 children
from six to fifteen,
under SS guns,
parading barefoot through
the ghetto of Terezin
to the delousing stage,

stumbling in rags,
their eyes haunted,
see the word *Gas,*
begin yelling and weeping,
won't enter,
have to be dragged.
Later, someone will say
they were from Bialystok,
that the SS shot their
mothers and fathers
before their eyes.
Within a few months
most will die of typhus.

After The Transport

A guard with the
special detail,
seeing the wife of his friend
in the undressing room,
comes right out and tells her
what is about to happen:
that she'll be exterminated,
be ashes in three hours.
She believes him
and runs all over
warning the other women,
We are going to be killed,
gassed! Mothers carrying
babies on their shoulders
don't want to hear that,
decide she is crazy,
chase her away.
When no one will listen
she starts to scream,

scratches her face to ribbons
out of shock and despair.
Everyone is gassed.
The woman is held back.
They torture her terribly
because she won't
betray the guard.
In the end she points to him.
He is thrown alive
into the oven.

Arrivals At Little Camp

Sometimes
under pressure of blows
they break suddenly
into movement
like a herd of cattle
jostling each other.
You can not get them
to say their names
or the date of their birth.
Even kindness can not
make them speak.
They look at you with
a long expressionless stare.
If they try to answer,
their tongues cannot reach
their dried up palates
to make a sound.
You are aware only
of a poisonous breath
appearing to come from
entrails already in a state
of decomposition.

One SS Man's Whip

The people are beaten
getting their hair cut off.
They are crowded in,
no water.
Then they are whipped again.
Always more blows.
Women to the left,
men to the right!
More blows.
Go in there—strip!
Always whipped. Always
running and screaming.
That is how they are
finished off.

Men's Barracks
At Sachseahausen
Concentration Camp

Five hundred to a thousand
in a single bunk,
the building infested
with fleas, rats.
Whistles at dawn
for the rag clad inmates.
If a bit of soup is
spilled over, prisoners
will huddle at the spot,
dig their spoons
into the mud,
stuff the mess
into their mouths.
Dysentery is epidemic

but prisoners are denied
access to latrines.
Clothing, bunks and floors
are soiled, spread disease.
One who survives
will later write,
They condemned us
to die in our own filth,
destroyed our human dignity,
filled us with horror
and contempt for ourselves
and our fellows.

Notebook

When completely destroyed
in the soul, people dream . . .
Thousands lie on
plank beds and dream.
The old, dragged
from hospital beds,
skin and bones, starved,
dragged out in the night . . .
Children are thrown
like puppets
through windows . . .
New symptoms of hunger:
pain in the nails and toes . . .
On the street,
women sit on a stone step
and eat red soup,
slurp and suck,
drink,
tip the bowl
to lap up the last drop . . .

Potato Peels

Given by doctor's
prescription
before starvation.
People walk with sunken
black or grey cheeks,
glaring eyes,
dragging along
like a cursed ghost
driven into courtyards
where garbage is piled
for a piece of potato
that can still be licked,
a rag that once wrapped food
and can still be
gnawed at,
live out their last days
up to their necks in garbage.

Soup Bowls

No one is without a bowl.
An administrator
comes home from the office,
presses his briefcase
against his body
and his soup bowl.
A worker goes home
from his job,
his soup bowl swinging
along with his tools.
Six, eight, ten women
pull a cart with waste;
as many bowls bang

against the cart.
Men drag a cart of the dead,
soup bowls hanging from
their back sides.
A woman who has
just washed her hair,
made up her face
with the last bit of cream,
takes her purse,
her soup bowl.
Children on the way to
the co-op take a bowl,
in case. When thousands
are deported from the ghetto,
the only thing they can take
is their bowl.

Toilet Facilities
In Place Duscielny

Open sitting boards.
In the entrance
and in the room itself—
piles of shit, puddles of urine.
A well-cared-for woman's hand
holds the door, in case one
mistakenly tries to open it.
Everything is congested
with dreck.
Used toilet paper
sticks to one's shoes and
is carried into the courtyard
where in one corner or another
some relieve themselves
in the light.

In The Coal Mines

Young girls step out of
the one dress they own,
go naked into the pit,
in seconds are
covered with mud.
Boys and girls
get to know the secrets
of their mothers and fathers
right there.
They take care of
bodily needs in full view.
No time for amenities.

Agenda

Women without periods.
Complete death of the erotic,
especially among western Jews.
Thus, no marriages.

Before The Red Cross
Comes To Inspect

New linens are given out,
nurses get fresh uniforms.
A few barracks are
scrubbed and painted.
All orphans are shipped east
(those with TB to Auschwitz);
they keep the pretty girls.
Jack boots and side arms
are locked up for the day.

Houses are painted pastel.
Shouldering rakes,
a squad of singing Jewish girls
marches off to tend gardens.
White gloved bakers unload
fresh bread into a fake store.
Fresh vegetables are displayed
for the first and last time.
In the community center
Terezin's orchestra plays Mozart.
A goal is scored
according to script
as the inspectors approach
a soccer field.
Children in clean clothes
play on a merry-go-round.
One Jew wears a pressed suit
and is chauffeured around
by an SS man
who, the day before,
kicked and beat him.

The Actors

A Dutch Jew,
a former film director,
is ordered to make a film:
*The Führer Presents the Jews
with a City.*
He cannot say no
so he begins a script
using the theme of water—
rivers, baths, faucets,
showers, irrigation.
Camera men come from Berlin.

Only a few people are
willing to be in the film.
Most drift away.
There is another problem:
Berlin has decreed that
only prisoners who *look*
like Jews can appear.
They must be hook nosed,
dark haired, dark eyed,
and furtive. However,
Terezin is filled with
blonde haired blue eyed Jews.
One sequence
showing a track meet
presents a crisis:
the high jump champion
from Czechoslovakia, a Jew,
is forbidden to participate;
she has blonde hair.

The Script

*We have just received
orders from the authorities
indicating that
a football match
between the League Victors
and the Trophy Winners
will be filmed tomorrow
at 3 p.m. For this we need
exactly 3,000 spectators.
Exact directions can only be
issued tomorrow morning
and will be determined
by the weather.*

150 copies printed from Bell and Stymie types to mark the poet's visit to Toledo during the month of November 1997.

Reeds in snow

lyn lifshin

aureole press 1997

like women with long
hair running out of
a burning building
dazed, half frozen
from a hotel room
of clothes and rings
from dead relatives
or a hand written
manuscript there's
no other copy of

LYN
the
LIFSHIN
creative
BLUE
process
TATTOO

Lyn Lifshin's **Blue Tattoo** *presents chilling graphic images of the Holocaust experience. Yet Ms. Lifshin is neither a Holocaust survivor nor is she the child of survivors. She was, in fact, born in Burlington, Vermont—a decade after the horrors which resulted in World War II.*

Blue Tattoo *is a collection of poems dealing with the various stages of anti-Jewish sentiment in Europe during the 1930's, culminating in the Holocaust. Often written from a first-person point of view, like letters or diaries, the poems are immediate, intense and accessible. Their presentation in* **Blue Tattoo,** *with its narrow columns set in type faces from the era, reads like fragments of war news transmitted from the front lines.*

Event Horizon Press recently asked Ms. Lifshin to describe how she became involved in writing about the Holocaust, what her relationship is to the Holocaust, and how she has undertaken writing poetry about it.

As many know, I am not a survivor, nor am I a child of survivors. Growing up Jewish, I heard my mother's accounts of roommates in the mostly non-Jewish college from which she graduated. The roommates would say such things as, "Hitler is right, Frieda, but *you* are different."

The summer I was six, a baby sitter told me taless of what happened in tunnels to Jewish children during World War II. She told me of the torture, the ovens. I slept fitfully for that whole year, and often woke up screaming. The stories had entered my dreams, my nightmares, and kept me dreaming of fire over and over. From that time on, I have been haunted and fascinated by the many narratives I heard from those who were actually involved. I was stunned when I first saw the film *Night and Fog* in the '60s, and since then have absorbed as many anecdotes as I could—reports from survivors, stories in films, diaries, and journals, interviews, radio discussions, books, magazine and newspaper articles. I went to museums and exhibits, viewed countless films, and took notes for years, filling my own journals with the chronicles, and trying to capture the speaking voices, just as they told their incredible histories.

Over the years, people have called to tell me their long, long narratives, have asked me to retell their parents' tales, and begged me to write down what they were telling, in order to keep their words and lives alive.

As a poet who writes about diverse subjects, I'm often asked to lead writing workshops on many things: feelings about war, mothers and daughters, feelings about women's sexuality and sensuality. I do workshops about writing the story of one's life, the urban ghetto, about diaries and journals, and about writing from the inside out and the outside in—with an emphasis on using museums, exhibits and the lives of others as creative impetus.

When I was asked to do a workshop about

Writing Through the Holocaust, in combination with an exhibit and with Holocaust survivors involved, I felt inadequate knowing only the stories of others. But I wanted to bring the reality of the Holocaust—the actual words and feelings and experiences of those who had gone through what they had gone through—to my students, many of whom were not Jewish, many of whom were young. My main aim was one I feel is the same as that most desired by those who perished and those who survived the Holocaust: that their words and experiences not be forgotten. I wanted my students to be close—to get as deeply as possible into the lives and feelings of those who underwent the atrocities and told of them in their own words. I stressed these words to my students through the voluminous notes I had taken.

Over time these words became part of my poems: not with the intention of using the lives and deaths as art for its own sake, but to use art as a means of keeping the reality of the words alive. When planning a workshop, I would take armfuls of books from the library, fifty books at a time, and then go back for more. Friends sighed that I talked and thought of nothing else. I jotted down passages to share with my students, passages to trigger their own poems. These were writing workshops, not history workshops, and it was the passion and feeling, the life experiences, I fervently wanted the students to comprehend.

When Event Horizon Press contacted me about doing a book of Holocaust poems to be published on the fiftieth anniversary of Victory in Europe Day, I sent the editors over a thousand poems. These were derived from readings, interviews, dreams, museum visits, telephone calls, photographs, films, videos, fantasies, surrealistic free-flow, panel discussions, conversations with survivors, stories others told me of their discussions with survivors, letters, exhibits, writing with students in workshops, discussions with soldiers who liberated the camps, African American soldiers, Jewish American soldiers, news reports, radio accounts, children born to survivors in Israel . . .

The process of creativity is one of things merging, being telescoped and braided together with—hopefully—proficiency, imagination, and devices of the craft. Since I am only an *observer* of the Holocaust, the feelings, words and impressions I have set down in the poems must, by their very nature, be ultimately attributed to others.

It would be impossible to pinpoint attributions for each poem in **Blue Tattoo**. A historian recently told me that some of the passages and images are derived from accounts in *Lodz Ghetto: Inside a Community Under Siege*, edited by Alan Adelson and Robert Lapides. She also noted sources such as Robert Azbug's *Inside The Vicious Heart* and *The Art of the Holocaust*, as well as the films *Shoah* and *Hotel Terminus*.

So—the voices in **Blue Tattoo** are based on the voices of those who were involved in the Holocaust. I know some people believe that one who has not participated directly in the Holocaust should not write about it. Others feel that poetry and fiction should not come from these experiences. But I feel that keeping the memory alive, relating the experiences and the suffering, and drawing upon the real words of real people who knew the Holocaust firsthand, is a legitimate way to remember and honor those who were its victims.

This collection of poetry is assembled in the spirit of countless survivors who intoned, "Lest they forget," as they painfully told of their experiences. As a member of the surviving Jewish culture, though not literally a Holocaust survivor, for me their anthem translates "Lest *we* forget." I will continue to do workshops to assure that we do not.

Lyn Lifshin

We consider it important
that there are many
young persons among
the spectators, but please,
no old people under any
circumstances.

For A Film About How Good Terezin Is For The Jews

Food rations are tripled.
The Tales of Hoffman
is performed at a staged
pleasant garden party.
A train bearing Jewish
children from Holland
is met by a band.
When the film is done,
the concerts stop.
Dancing is forbidden.

Auschwitz Artists

Scavenged empty
toothpaste tubes
from officers' garbage bins
are used to store
pilfered paints.
Brushes are made
of human hair,
straw or feathers
(or hairs discreetly plucked
from the fur coats

of Nazi visitors).
Artists in the woods use twigs,
even blades of grass
old SS circulars,
target papers full of
bullet holes.

Twins In Auschwitz 1

When the train stops,
just smoke and flame.
They don't know
what the fire means.
Tall barbed wire.
Their mother holds them,
frozen in place.
They ask her two times,
Are they twins?
She doesn't know
if it is good.
The third time she says *Yes.*
They shove her
in one direction,
yank them in the other.
She doesn't want to let go.
They hear a horrible scream.

Twins In Auschwitz 2

On the first day
their skin is tattooed,
injections begun.
I don't know what they used,
but I couldn't walk.

They took pieces out of me,
X-rayed, cut more.
They see bodies
fall into pits.
Some are still alive.
After awhile
it seems normal.

Twins In Auschwitz 3

They are saved
to be tortured.
Mengele?
He did not look mean
until you saw his eyes,
a monster
in the skin of a lamb.
His eyes, cold lakes.
Oh yes,
saved to be tortured.
They cut and stitched
and cut me open again.
They don't cut twins' hair.
If one twin dies
they will kill the other.

Twins In Auschwitz 4

There is always smoke.
Four stacks of fire.
When the transports come
they burn all night.
A skeletal woman
staggers toward them,

asks where they came from.
Do you know where
my babies are?
A guard sees,
sends a German Shepherd
after her.
It tears her to pieces.

Klein Festung

SS men force prisoners
to load wheelbarrows
by picking up
mouthfuls of dirt,
use Jews as targets,
beat and kick prisoners,
starve many to death.

After News
Of 55 Escapees

The Bürger
orders a census.
Mist and drizzle.
40,000 prisoners
march to a muddy field,
stand all day
without food or water,
no toilets,
bending, weeping,
murmuring, fainting.
Airplanes overhead,
machine guns

in the mountains.
Toward evening
children shriek,
the old and ill collapse.
Many die.
The census goes on
from 7 a.m. until midnight,
establishing nothing.
After midnight
the Jews are allowed
to stagger back
over 300 corpses.

That Sunday

The guards make everyone
slap the prisoner
pulled with a rope
pale, naked, barefoot.
At first no one moves.
The guards get a whip.
Then hundreds of palms
slap the prisoner.
His face is swollen.
The guards make everyone
stop slapping him.
His face swelling,
his eyes hidden,
he begs to be hit harder
so he can die soon.
He passes out, falls.
The guards try to revive him,
shake him, bring out
a pail of water
to dash on his face.

When he doesn't move
they hoist the victim
into a sitting position,
splash gasoline into his armpits,
lift his arms high
and strike a match.
Flames flash.
The burning brings
the prisoner to.
Before the flames
catch in his hair
the guards
water down the fire.
They pull him to his feet
by the choker rope
shortened to one foot.
Suddenly the ranks break loose.
The guards get nervous,
drop the chunk of
swollen blood,
reach for their guns
to restore order.
By the time they
get back to the man
it is over for him.

The Song

Overlooking a quarry
where hundreds of Dutch Jews
have been forced to jump
from a high cliff
to their death,
an SS officer orchestrates
a blasting operation

that makes even
jaded prisoners tremble:
he orders an Italian Jew
known to have a beautiful voice
to stand on a rock mound
and sing the *Ave Maria*.
As he sings, charges
are laid around the rocks.
In mid-song the officer
presses the plunger
and blasts the rocks
and the Jew
with dynamite.

At Thekla

Ruins, corpses, charred bodies.
The SS lures the prisoners
into one of the barracks
with big pots of soup,
obstructs the doors,
nails heavy army blankets
over the windows,
brings in huge containers
of flammable acetate,
douses the interior
and the prisoners,
locks the doors
and ignites the building
with rifle fire
and hand grenades.
Those who attempt escape,
bodies on fire,
are shot, beaten to death,
impaled on a fence

and machine gunned.
Some victims
are so close to freedom
that a Polish professor,
his body on fire,
manages to squeeze himself
halfway through
the outer fence,
the shriveled
lower half of his body
ashes on one side,
his head unharmed—
even his glasses in place.

Before Each Gassing

Strict precautions:
The crematorium
is surrounded by SS
patrolling the courtyard
with dogs and machine guns.
To the right are steps
that lead underground
to the undressing rooms,
then to a room where
three thousand
can be gassed at one time.

In Treblinka

A pit of corpses.
Children who come alone
are led to a big red cross,
a sign *The Infirmary*,
where they are shot.

In The Dressing Room

Signs in several languages:
Clean is fine.
Lice can kill.
Wash yourself.
To the Disinfectant Area.
All to lure the people
into the gas chambers
already undressed.

Blue Tattoo

On each arm
a seven-digit number.
It hurts a little
as the flesh is pricked.
Blue fog.
Men are made to run barefoot
on blue iced snow at dawn.
Hydrogen cyanide.
Bluish pellets of Zyklon B gas,
effective in large rooms.
Men, women, children, babies,
stripped, crowded,
packed into the chamber.
Blue fog.
Families holding hands
stiffened in death,
no room to fall down.
It is difficult
to tear them apart
to empty the chamber
for the next load,
for more blue tattoos.

On The Way To The Shower

Some women
take out soap and towels,
assured,
entering the barbers' rooms,
they are going to baths.
They stand naked
awaiting their turns
in bitter frost
as children's bare feet
freeze to the earth.

On The Way To The Gas

The woman is naked,
her damp hair
in strings.
The SS officer leers
Don't you dance?
and orders her
to dance for him.
She does,
and as she dances
moves closer to him,
grabs his gun
and shoots him.
Although she too
is quickly shot,
she dies dancing—
a dancer,
not a number
without a name.

Death Panic

The women waiting
hear motors
of the gas chambers,
people begging and screaming.
As they wait
death panic overtakes them.
Death panic
makes people let go.
They empty themselves
from the front or rear.
Often where the women stand
there are five or six
rows of excrement.

Once The Gas
Is Poured In

It spreads upward
from the floor of the chamber.
Prussic acid fumes
from Zyklon B pellets
first hit the smallest
and weakest,
and in the terrible struggle
the lights are switched off.
No one can see,
and in their agony
the strongest people
climb on top of
the dead bodies on the floor
realizing the higher they climb
the more air there is.
Or they try to push

their way to the door,
push their way out.
A death struggle.
This is why the youngest
and old
are always at the bottom.
Even there,
the strongest on top.
A father doesn't recognize
his son lies below him.
Then they fall out,
like stones from a truck.

The Red Trillium

Red Trillium
poking up
through thick leaves
dark as menstrual blood
pooling at the bottom
when they open
the gas chambers,
the bodies frozen,
merging,
leaning toward an
imagined light:
a family fused
in the claws of each other,
a daughter climbing
her mother's side,
up past her shoulders
as she did as a baby,
as if the little air left
would help her
hold on.

Death March

Five days before
the Russians break through,
Warsaw prisoners are sent
on a 100 mile death march,
ending up in Dachau.
Those who cannot
keep walking are shot,
their corpses left
on the side of the road.
There is no food, no water.
240 survive of 3,600.
Yet there is hope
to the last breath.
They are still hoping
and praying
as they are marched
into the gas chamber.

Edward R. Murrow

If you are having lunch,
or not up to it,
turn off your radio.
It was Buchenwald.
There was an evil-smelling
hoard; death had already
marked many.
There was applause.
It was the clapping of babies.
Some fell out of bed.
Some were crawling
to the latrine.
I won't describe it.

I saw children
who rolled up their sleeves
and showed me their numbers.
Professors from Poland,
doctors from all over,
crawled to reach me,
touched me.
Then we saw the bodies—
stacked like cord wood.
There was little flesh.
They were so white.
I think there were over 500,
neatly stacked.
Then there was another
German trailer with 250
starved or shot.
I pray you to believe
what I have said about
Buchenwald.
I have reported
what I saw and heard,
but only part of it.
For much, I have no words.
If I have offended you
by this rather mild account,
I am not in the least sorry.

Treblinka

It is green and still
after forty years.
Then, nothing.
No one left to bear witness.
It is a silence
where nothing moves.

Idyll

Once it inspired
landscape paintings,
enchanted by gentle
greens and yellows
that shimmered
in the misty light.
Even in 1945,
American soldiers
entering the town
see flower beds,
trees, small shrubs,
churches with steeples,
a mirrorlike river . . .
a few feet away
from the firing squads,
and the rooms where victims
were made to eat salt water,
were injected with malaria,
were left in freezing water
until their lungs burst.

Nordhausen

What this was all about
didn't sink in
until we got to Nordhausen,
says one American soldier.
Barracks of dead bodies.
Two thousand townspeople
are forcibly enlisted
for the burial work.
From the bodies they
try to pick out those

that still show signs of life.
The German civilians were
as sick as our guys were.
The stink. We went numb,
thought of them as creatures.
The soldiers could not
deal with seeing anyone
brutalized to such a state.

Odors

Oh! The odors!
There is no way to describe
the odors!
Many of the boys
I am talking about
were tough soldiers,
combat men who had been
all the way through invasion.
They were ill, vomiting,
from the odors!

Gunskirch

Of all the horrors of the place
the smell is the most startling:
excrement, foul body odors,
smoldering trash fires,
German tobacco
(a stink in itself)
all fused together
in a thick, muddy woods—
the ground pulpy,
mixed with shit and urine,

churned to warm putty
by thousand of feet.
As the soldiers enter the camp
the living skeletons who
are still able to walk
crowd around them,
insane with hunger.
The very sight of an American
brings cheers, groans
and shrieks.
People crowd in,
want to touch an American,
touch their Jeeps,
kiss their arms
to make sure it is true!
Those who can't walk
crawl toward the Jeeps.
Those who can't crawl
prop themselves on an elbow
and somehow
through their pain and suffering
reveal through their eyes
the gratitude and joy
they feel seeing
Americans.

Chocolate

There are SS troops
trying to shoot people
who are trying to leave.
Some are crawling, on fire,
over bodies that have been shot.
Skin and bones,
they look like skeletons.

A soldier gives one
a piece of chocolate,
but his officer says,
Don't feed—you'll kill them.

The Stack

The first thing
the soldier sees
is a stack of bodies
about twenty feet long,
as high as a man can reach.
It looks like cord wood.
What the soldier
will never forget
is that looking closer
there are people
whose eyes are still blinking
maybe three or four deep
inside the stack.

Ordruf

Men with eyes that are dark,
holes in their skull and face;
dead scattered in piles
or on the open ground;
a butcher's block
used to smash gold fillings
from the mouths of the dead;
the living and the dead
in double-decker barracks
three to a bunk, half-hidden
in mounds of excrement.

Bergen Belsen

As the British take over,
behind the attractive main gate
they find piles of bodies
flung into a truck
by German prisoners—as if
they were dumping garbage.
A hundred prisoners
crawl toward the troops
in the hope they have food.
In the barracks an animal cry
pierces the silence,
then one hears only
the steady drip, drip
of excrement—
from one tier of bunks
to the next, to the ground.

Mauthausen

The liberators cheer!
And the liberated?
Some celebrate, some try,
while others hardly know
what has happened
before they die.

Dachau Liberation

Some prisoners
hoist their liberators
in the triumph
and carry them across
the parade ground,
while others cheer
and kiss the surprised GI's.
Someone manages to
make an American flag
which he waves wildly.
Some barracks are painted
with triumphant slogans.
One celebrant becomes
so excited that he bolts
from the barracks
and becomes electrocuted
on the wires of the fence.

Ebensee Survivors

Some walk around
naked in a daze;
others are wrapped
in blankets held closed
with a belt.
Their facial features
are normal,
everything else is
completely
out of proportion.

Woebblin

Seeing the skinny people
clinging to life,
and having nothing
but candy bars,
a soldier gives one

to a man who runs away
gulping it, trying to swallow it
before someone takes it
from him, choking
into unconsciousness.

Americans!

Some were too weak,
too close to death.
They'd ask, Americanish?
We'd say Yeah,
and some of them
would get up, stand up,
and some would fall back.
They were skin and bones.

Buchenwald Liberation

The living, the near dead
and the dead:
stacked on shelves.
At the sight of American
uniforms a horde of gnomes
pours out of doorways
as if shot from a cannon.
Some hop on crutches,
some hobble on stumps of feet.
All wear striped
convict suits
or gray black patches
of clothing.
Some are crying.
Others shout with joy.

What The Soldiers See At Liberation

Cadaverous refugees,
feverish sunken eyes,
shaved skulls.
People buried
in a big hole.
Someone moans
in broken German.
In through the gates
lies a pile of dead prisoners
in striped uniforms.
The corpses are fleshless;
at the back of each skull
is a bullet hole.
A shed is stacked with
stiff naked men,
the bodies flat and yellow
as lumber.

Mass Graves

The soldier said
I didn't feel anything,
Nothing at all. Just gasped
Jesus Christ, Jesus Christ.
I kept saying that to myself
because I couldn't think
of anything else.
It didn't seem like these
were people. They were
so thin and dried out
they might have been paper
or plaster of paris.

The Bedroom

Near the only toilet,
an open concrete ditch,
a three year old child
lies on a rotting
lice-covered mattress,
surrounded by piles of
half-burned bodies.

Symbols

The children eat whatever
the soldiers give them.
The soldiers get clothes
from another town.
More than 220 children
are still alive.
The new clothes are
mysterious; with pride
they put them on.
The sweaters and skirts
are symbolic, mean new hope.
The soldiers cannot believe
that humans have done this.

Buchenwald's
Little Camp
At Liberation

The men are so emaciated
their joints bulge.
Their loins are smeared
with their own shit.

If they move at all
it is a crawl, a slowness
that makes them look like
huge lethargic beetles.
Many lie in their bunks
as if dead. In response
to pleas for food,
an American pulls
a chocolate bar
from his pocket.
Galvanized into motion,
the men clutch for the bar
wildly. One reaches it,
others pounce on him—
the brown melting in
filthy hands, then gone.

Ebensee Liberation

The bodies are like
hides and carcasses
one might see hanging
in a butcher shop;
Every vertebrae,
every rib, visible.
These are the dead,
and the living
look just like them.

Ashes

There is a big pit
stacked with bodies, wood.
I'll never forget the ashes,

says one soldier.
It looked like a whole hip
burning, and I touched it
with a stick and it just
fell apart.

The Ovens

You can see they were used
24 hours; they have
broken down.
They burned them,
sold their ashes,
sold their dentures.
I knew about lynching
but I didn't know
about Nazis.

Natzwiller

A large pile of hair,
appearing and reputed
to be female,
an incineration room,
an autopsy room,
and in the cellar
four coffins and
a sheet metal elevator
which would take
a human being
with stains
that appeared to be
caused by
blood.

Behind A Wall

Hair cut from the oven,
bound,
packed in 40 pound bales
for stuffing mattresses,
making socks.
At the liberation
of Auschwitz,
Soviets find
15,000 pounds.

Soldier At Dachau

Before we got here
some said it was
propaganda,
that it wasn't as bad
as they said.
When I got to Buchenwald,
well, even though
I witnessed it,
it is hard to tell anyone.
I was dazed.
It could not have happened,
I thought,
in a country like
Germany.
There were bodies
still on hooks,
fingernails
embedded in
stone walls
from where their fingers
had dug in.

The Experiments

In another part
there were jars
full of pieces of people.
Weird experiments.
People gutted like a deer.
Refrigerators full of bodies,
stacks of them,
that had been left in the cold
to see how long it took
to freeze people.

Even The Liberators
Feel Like Victims

They dream of capture,
of falling through bodies
up to their hips in mud,
numbers tattooed on skin,
hair on fire or in a pile,
bodies seeming to be
trying to move, to run—
but frozen, mouths open
in a final shriek.

With The War Ending

We were taken from
Bergen Belsen
to be gassed in Poland.
It was spring, 1945.
It was April,
the tenth of April.

Thirteen days in cattle cars.
Each morning they would
throw out the corpses.
Of 2,500, 675 died.
Then the train was stopped
in the middle of the night
in the middle of the forest.
Someone screamed in Russian;
a Russian Jewish general.
The starved Jews
rushed to a nearby village
and over ate.
200 dropped dead.
At night the Russian soldiers
raped the Jewish women
in front of their husbands.

Liberation

With the Allies near
the Nazis locked us
in a building,
set dynamite charges.
But it rained,
so nothing went off.
I was 68 pounds,
my hair snow.
When the first American came
I said, I am Jewish.
He said he was, too,
held the door open,
and in that gesture
five years of being
hostage at gun point, dirt,
he restored my humanity.

With American Planes Surrounding Us

The Germans got nervous.
There was a heap of corpses.
I was found near this heap.
For the first time in my life
I saw new uniforms,
black faces.
I'd heard about
this country,
America.
I saw the Americans
as angels.

A Black Soldier's Story

I saw people
who were skeletons
holding each other,
talking in languages
I'd never heard.
One man's hands were
webbed together
in malnutrition.
When they started to
move toward me
I backed away.
Then I thought,
What could be their crime?
A man who spoke English
came and began to tell me
that because they weren't
good enough to live
they'd been brought here.

A Japanese American Liberates Dachau

They were so skinny
you couldn't tell the difference
between a man and a woman.
There I was at Dachau,
and I thought,
My own wife and children
are behind barbed wire.
A Dachau survivor said
You don't look like
what I thought Americans
would look like.
I got down on my knees
and swore to my God
I was there to save them.

Buchenwald

When the soldiers came
it was like angels.
People were covered with
pieces of blankets.
Some were clinging to life.
Some stretched hands:
Brother, give me your hand—
I am dying.
And then I saw
the soldiers cry.
I didn't know why
they were crying.
I hadn't cried
all the time
in Buchenwald.

At Dachau

The clocks are set at
the same time they were
when the liberators arrived.
When the Americans came,
this tall guy,
I thought he was an angel
that came from the moon.
I didn't know
whether to hug him.
I couldn't talk.
I just held my hand out.

After Liberation

The Army made the Germans
see what they had done.
Chandeliers of human skin.
I was about fifty pounds.
A big black soldier
lifted me up, said
Look, this is your enemy.
I was so proud to be
held and lifted up.
I thought they were angels.

March 1945

I went to this house
and saw Germans
come to the door.
I saw a big German officer.
Surrender, *I ordered.*

He said,
I won't surrender to a nigger.
I hit him across the mouth,
saw teeth fly.

Afterward

He said it was a dream
within a dream,
even after chocolate and wine,
even when bread
didn't have to be clawed at,
he was still on the verge,
still waiting.
He didn't know how
he'd start over, find energy.
He felt empty, heavy.
Years were a parenthesis.
At first he couldn't sleep.
Trains going in separate,
splitting directions.
How they'd held out,
mysterious,
tinged with shame;
what was longed for
muddled, muffled.
Nothing could happen
to rub out the scars.
It was thawing outside.
The smell of filth and death.
Dazed, in a blur,
drizzle fog blur,
a Christmas tree the gallows
as he was being lifted
onto a cart,

jostled through fields
he'd passed near to
years before,
to go back home
still in a dream
inside a dream
where the colors go,
and he's snatched back
into gray chaos
and knows only
this is not the reprieve,
the escape from—
nothing else is true.

Especially Around
The Holidays

It hits.
I was in a concentration camp.
It was 50 years ago,
but now—
Passover, Mother's Day—
I have terrible dreams
about my family.
If I go to sleep at eleven
I'm drenched by twelve.
I don't even want to
go to sleep.
It was on Mother's Day
my mother was gassed.
My father was thrown
into the water,
my brother shot.
But it is my own children
in these dreams,

as if
what happened then
is still going on.

Her First Memory
Of Camp

Sitting in a chair
and having her head shaved,
mingling with her tears.
Then a uniform
is shoved at her,
and a pair of clogs
as she is pushed outside.
And they handed me this,
she frowns,
clutching her uniform,
to me, Fritzi,
a pampered child
this itchy gray—
and then,
into the snake pit!

For Years
Her Parents Never Said
A Word About It

After my brothers
and sisters were
killed they decided
never to mention
the Holocaust,
or the aunt who lived
long enough to sort

through clothes and
belongings to find
the wedding gown
of a murdered sister.
But now everything
sparks a memory.
Only a year ago
Mother put up,
next to my picture
in her bedroom,
a photograph, she says,
Of my first daughter.

Chelmno

When I saw all I saw
I wasn't affected.
I was thirteen.
All I'd seen was death.
It was normal.
Walk a hundred yards
in the ghetto
and there would be
two hundred bodies.
Sons took their
fathers' bread;
fathers took their sons'.
By Chelmno,
I didn't care about anything.
If I survived
I wanted just one thing:
five loaves of bread.
I was sure if I got out,
I'd be the only one
left in the world.

Silent Night

We were hidden
in the Catholic orphanage.
Christmas of '44.
It was white, snow falling,
but we had warmth
from extra coal,
larger food portions,
even mail.
A tree in the corner.
We children were seated
on both sides of a long table,
singing Christmas carols—
their simple, pleasant message
totally out of context
with the savage war
that had raged
six Christmases.
Food in our stomachs
loosened our tongues
and unlike the usual silence
enforced during meals
we were told stories.
Suddenly the door opened
and a German officer came in.
Children, *Mother Superior said,*
the Commander of the
German garrison in Zelnia
is a devout Catholic
and he asked to spend
the evening with you.
As we started to sing
Silent Night,
I wondered,
Even on this night

must the Germans intrude
on the tiny and shaky?
When we finished,
a pause,
and the Commandant
whispered to Mother Superior.
After a moment's hesitation
she asked, Is there
anyone here who can sing
Silent Night in German?
It will make our guest happy.
My sister and I knew German;
we learned the German
version of this song
before the Slovak one.
But I wasn't sure I should
stand up and sing it
for our enemy.
Then I saw my sister rise
and the decision
had been made for me.
So I stood beside her.
As we sang,
the face above the medals
became animated,
the lips moved with our words.
Then, suddenly,
my sister gasped
and realized what I feared:
Why are we
the only two who know
the German version?
The officer has trapped us,
he knows we are Jewish.
He motioned us to approach.
It seemed forever

before he spoke.
Then, looking at us,
he softly said in German,
Don't be afraid.
Your mother and father
will come back.
For him, too,
it was a silent night.

Gift Of The Raspberry

Don't poison your day,
she smiles,
her black eyes bright.
Use the beacon of the past,
the darkness,
to outline the present
that we often take
for granted.
I saw in the work camp
beauty: my friend,
though starving,
fifty pounds,
found a raspberry—
kept it in her pocket all day
for me.
What kept me going?
It was the memory
of the ordinary day,
the kind I'd, then,
have thought boring.
It was all I dreamt of
behind barbed wire.
Days after the gift
of the raspberry

Sasha gave me
the biggest gift:
on the Death March
she begged,
unable to go on,
though I could have
curled up next to her,
that I must go on.

Doorbells

When they left,
Mother was crying
with relief, with terror.
She cradled herself
against my stunned
little brother.
I turned away.
I swore I would do
something other than cry.
I began to pick up clothes
when the doorbell
rang again.
It was Father.
I have two minutes.
Mother said What?
But she knew.
His eyes had become glass;
there was another crew
waiting downstairs.
They gave me two minutes.
Now Father
was the only one not crying,
his eyes blue glass
his kiss stubbly.

If I don't come back—
avenge me.
Gone.
His fingers stung,
burning into my skin
a sense of continuity
against all odds.
I stopped crying.
Four months later he
rang our doorbell twice,
skull shaven, skeletal,
released from Dachau,
somehow alive.
Forty years later, today,
he is practicing the tango
with Mother in Miami Beach.
My little brother is
chairman of political science.
We are atypically lucky.
But to this day
we all ring
our American doorbells
twice.

After Kristallnacht

We said we couldn't believe
anything like this
could happen in 1938.
It took awhile to sink in.
Then I saw people pulled,
chased into the ghetto;
saw naked women running,
just a pad between their legs.
I kept a curtain down.

Later, in the Ukraine,
I saw a huge hole.
Naked bodies lining up.
It took me awhile to realize
this was extermination.
1,800 shot.
It didn't occur
until after the war
that we were new witnesses
to something of humanity
being destroyed.
It is my responsibility
and guilt
that I am alive.

Stefanya, A Polish Girl

I was 16 years old.
My parents had been
carried out to labor camps.
We had little food.
I'd seen a whole family
hanged for hiding Jews,
but I had to help—
to share our few crumbs.
People keep asking me
why I could have risked
hiding so many.
My parents told me,
It doesn't matter,
when it comes to people.
If you can help,
don't hesitate.
It doesn't matter
about money or religion.

There is one God.
When I saw what
the SS was doing,
I knew it was terribly wrong.
One man came,
asked for one night of shelter.
He had jumped from
a running train that was
on the way to a camp.
Even after the Gestapo
took over part of our rooms,
my six year old sister
and I had to help.
Who else will teach humanity
if they see only killing?
Soon we were hiding
thirteen people.
After two years of terror
we were liberated.
We all survived.
Then Joseph,
one I helped,
asked me to marry him.
He didn't want to leave me.

Did My Parents
Keep Quiet About It?

No. They didn't talk
about much else.
My own children are
five and three;
they'll come to me,
say Nanny told us.
We tell them it was

a long time ago
in a different country,
that no one should forget.
We have no photographs,
no faces for the names
that are only names,
though we've kept them alive
in the babies.
But although we're free here,
though we're never hungry,
never saw pogroms
never knew gas chambers—
my parents think,
always,
it is just a matter of time.

The Danes

He could remember
hiding under stinking canvas
in the hold of a fishing boat.
Nine year old Gustav
and his brothers were told
they must not cry out
or make a sound
if Nazis searched below deck
as the boat pulled out
into the sound.
Gustav's father
chanted a quiet prayer
under the canvas.
Two days earlier,
right before Rosh Hashanah,
men came with news
that Hitler had ordered

all Jews in Denmark
Rounded up and deported.
Overnight
the Danes organized,
hid families in homes
of non-Jewish neighbors
or strangers.
Night after night
small groups of Jews
were sneaked to shore
where they waded out
to fishing boats
to take them across the sound
to Sweden.
To Gustav,
now a lawyer
and part-time cantor,
freedom still smells like fish.
He remembers
the night the Gestapo came,
knocking and screaming
banging on doors,
trying keys,
until an upstairs neighbor
told them to stop screaming,
told them the Goldbergers
were away in the country.
The first rescue, he says.
With the water running
and the footsteps of children
they must have known
we were at home.
They escaped—
going to the country house,
returning when the danger
seemed over—

56

only to come back to news
that the Nazis would start
rounding up all Jews
the next day.
A Lutheran minister
gave them enough money
to pay the fishermen
(who hoped to provide
for their own families
in case of capture).
I remember waiting
in bushes on the beach
for the flash of light to signal
where the boat would be,
and wading out into
bitter cold water.
I screamed as it got deeper,
up to my neck.
After two hours in the hold
we climbed out and were
handed one by one
into a Swedish boat
cheering, singing!
After the war, Father
went back to Copenhagen;
found our home had
been cared for
by our Danish housekeeper.
Gustav looks at
yellowed clippings
of a singing group
he and his wife
created with their
four children;
she fingers a photo
of the young babies.

If the Danish rescue
had not happened,
that whole line of people
would never have existed.
When you save one person
you save the whole world.

He Had The Trains Run On Time

If there weren't
enough trainloads
it meant death for those
in the special details.
We saw thousands
and thousands
of innocents disappear
up the chimney.
We couldn't remember
what it meant to be human.
Train smoke, chimney smoke
the only hope
of escaping this hell.

Strength

They took me through
a corridor of portraits
of Hitler and Goebbels,
then into a room of manacles
with spikes and metal
harnesses, knives.
Someone cracked my spine
tighter and tighter.

I lost my breath.
I was tortured nine days.
Stripped completely,
they put me into an ice bath,
my feet tied to a board,
my hands tied behind me.
They scooped ice on me.
I thought my lungs would burst
but we are tougher
than we think.

What The Resister's Widow Said

He was asked if he would
volunteer to blow up Hitler,
knowing he'd be killed too.
Give me 24 hours, *he said.*
He came home and his father
asked what he was
mulling over so.
Peter told him,
and his father said,
Yes, you must.
A man who doesn't
take such a chance
will never be happy
with himself.

What Another Resister's Widow Said

The war was good for marriage.
It brought out the best

and the worst in us both,
and you can't make too much
out of tiny things.
I didn't want the children
to know their father
was hanged
but when they asked
I told them.
Later I got the bill.
150 marks for the execution.

So Many Bodies All Over

In most massacres
it was the same:
the Jews were marched
to a remote site,
ordered to undress.
Our father did not want
to undress, said Rivka,
who survived despite a
bullet wound in her head.
He did not want
to stand naked
so they tore the clothing
from his body
and shot him.
Rivka watched as her
80 year old grandmother
was shot along with
the two children she held.
Father's sister also had
children in her arms,
and she was shot on the spot.

Rivka's younger sister
was the next to die.
She went up to the Germans
with one of her friends,
embracing one another.
Standing there naked,
she begged to be saved.
A German looked into her eye
and shot the two of them.
Then my second sister,
and finally it was my turn.
I felt the Germans
take the child from my arms.
The child cried out
and was shot immediately.
Then he aimed at me,
ordered me to watch,
turned my head around, shot.
I fell to the ground.
After the Germans left,
in the pit of bodies, she rose,
using her last strength to
climb to the top of the grave.
I didn't know the place.
So many bodies.
Not all of them dead.
But in their last suffering
they were like smoke;
they camouflaged me.

One Survivor

We knew so little.
The first thing they did
was take our radios.

After two months
in the hospital,
the man who liberated me
(and who I'd later marry)
mentioned Pearl Harbor.
I said, Pearl who?

After The Camps

Houses weren't where
they'd been; furniture, lace,
any diamond or ruby stolen.
No one could believe
it was as it was.
A long search for a father,
a daughter, a wife.
The barracks were set on fire.
Smoke stung—
even in the next town.
A woman cut off
the yellow star
on a sister's blouse.
A woman with
43 dead relatives says
It would take a column
in the New Israel Weekly
just to list the names.

I'm Not A Survivor,
No, A Manicurist

That was my cover in Warsaw.
I covered and stood watch
for my husband,

chief of civil resistance.
I always had my
manicuring tools with me.
It saved my life.
One time I went into
a man's apartment
to give him letters
from London.
He'd been arrested.
The Gestapo asked
the housekeeper,
Is this the manicurist?
Once I brought hot cocoa
and milk to some
children in the ghetto,
returned in tears.
Next day in broad daylight
those children came across
a German patrol
and were shot.

Being A Painter Saved My Life

They wanted someone
who could make a drawing,
a caricature of an SS man,
so they could give it to him
for his birthday.
Someone gave me a pencil
and I drew him running along
and using a foot scooter.
I think it was to some degree
quite dangerous
because he might consider it

a joke to belittle him.
But he liked it.
That's how I survived.

Mengele's White Glove

It's a very clear memory.
Mengele was standing there
with a white glove,
pointing this way and that.
This way, gas.
That way, work.
My first husband was selected
to go to the gas.
I was selected to go to work.
They told us to leave
our luggage on the train.
There was a line of men,
a line of women—
always five across,
because it was easier
for them to count.
When we went to
the work camp they told us
the smoke we saw
was from the bodies
of our families.

Mengele Humor

We were all shaved
bald headed.
We women.
We looked like monkeys.

When we went for disinfecting,
through the cold showers,
there was one woman
who was quite hairy,
and of course
she couldn't shave in there.
And the SS man said,
One of us needs a shave,
kind of kidding.
You know, I sat there,
my head shaved,
clutching a bobby pin.

They Did This In Auschwitz-Birkenau

The man rolls up his sleeve
to show a ragged greenish
tattoo. *I was sixteen,*
taken alone to do slave labor.
A week later my parents
and sister came
and were killed in
the gas chamber.
The man pulls out
a government identity card,
fingers it,
crushes it in his hand,
puts it to his forehead,
covers his eye with it,
gazes at the ceiling,
at the floor,
rolls his eyes,
sweats.
Auschwitz was so degrading.

I'm still not able
to talk about most of it.
I was transported to Warsaw
at the tail end of the
Warsaw Ghetto uprising
to destroy evidence:
burn bodies,
dynamite buildings,
save material
for the Eastern Front.
I was beaten, hungry, cold.
There was always fear
and knowing that
we wouldn't get out alive.
We were told by the Germans,
If we don't kill you
you will kill us.
That was the order of the day:
to kill as many people
as they could
unless they could
get some work out of them.

Special Detail

With no trains
we had no work, no food.
We were starved—
wanted to live
until the rebellion.
When we heard
a train coming
we just thought of food,
crackers and jam.
Even working in

the Treblinka factory
our lives depended
on the process,
on the slaughter.

Work Squads

Those in the work squads
thought they would survive,
but by January they
stopped receiving food.
They weren't shot
or gassed—
but starved.
When typhus broke out
they were left to die,
dropped like flies.
They stopped believing,
said an SS man.
We said,
You're going to live.
We almost believed it.
Lie enough and you
believe your lies.

No More Need

When the death roll
went down in the camp
it meant no need for
replacements, no work.
Even healthy Dutch
and Belgian Jews
went right into the ovens.

All the more reason,
a survivor says,
for resistance—
even if suicidal.

At The Ramp

Some didn't know,
put on makeup,
combed their hair.
Within an hour they'd
fall out of the ovens
like potatoes.
I was like someone
shipwrecked
but still alive.
I was told to use my hands
to dig for bodies.
The deeper I dug
The flatter the bodies.
They crumbled.
Anyone who said corpse
was beaten.
We had to call the bodies
puppets *or* shit.

Fifty Years Later

If you
he says
could lick
my heart
it would
poison you.

Even Before, With Her Long Hair, People Supposed If She Was Jewish, She Had Lice

First I thought
Barbie was friendly.
He was stroking a cat,
a gray cat, smiling,
said, in French,
I was pretty.
Then suddenly
he ripped off my
hair band,
wrapped my hair
around his hand,
and yanked me
by my hair
to the floor,
saying
he wanted the address
where my brothers
and sisters were.
I didn't know;
in Lyon, many were
rushed to the shelters.
He kicked me
over and over—
made my mother watch.

There Were Screams Through Double Doors

Some pretended
to not notice.

Barbie tortured
my father to death:
hung him by his feet,
tore off his skin,
dunked him in
boiling water,
in ammonia,
the ice bath.
He had third degree burns
all over his body.
He could not sit
or lie down.
No one treated him.
He died the third day.
He died so bravely
the others stood up
and sang The Marseilles
for him.

One Doctor Who Assisted The SS Said

I cut the flesh
of healthy young girls,
immersed bodies
of dwarfs and cripples
in calcium chloride
to preserve them,
or had them boiled
so the carefully prepared
skeletons
might safely reach
the Third Reich museum.
I can never erase
these memories.

What He Remembered

Civil servants counting up
heaps of eyeglasses,
dolls, empty shoes.
Uniformed officers
dining on vegetables
fertilized by human ashes,
washing their hands with
soap made of human fat,
sleeping peacefully
on mattresses stuffed with
hair of murdered women.

SS Officer In The Ghetto

After the war, he published
mountain climbing books.
He loved the sun, the pure air.
He never knew about
death camps, the ghetto.
I had no idea!
You overestimate my power.
I worked for three years,
yes—
the conditions were terrible,
but I didn't know,
was a small part.
The extermination
wasn't clear.
They worked for
self-preservation,
self-management.
It wasn't death.
It wasn't clear to me.

When She Heard Some Of The Blows Didn't Connect

Played back slow motion
under her now white hair
she twitches, remembers
the black boots.
So—if one didn't
step on her fingers
after they
kicked her in the kidneys
that no longer work,
and had their way
into her.
So—if one missed
its target, her nipples,
she'd wait for a knife
to her temple.
One eye never again
closed as it used to.
Kicked up mud
she sprawled in
is flung back,
the police laughing,
piggish,
with plump fräuleins
hugging them.
They could as well
be lifting steins
as clubs.
Acquitted—
though we saw it,
the colors of law,
a blue streaked with
rust and blood;

following orders—
although
in front of our eyes
it didn't happen.

There Are Trees Now

It looks like a serene
little forest where the
death camps used to be.
You would feel like
having a picnic there.
He went back to Belzed
to reclaim his family.
His mother, sister,
and her three children
died there in World War II.
There are no graves,
but he reached down
and in his hands gathered
a small amount of dirt
to take back to the U.S.
It was the first time
in fifty years
I felt close to my mother.

When I Went Back
To The Warsaw Ghetto

The house I was born in
is an empty lot.
I used my hands
to pick up dirt,
felt a pain

I have trouble describing:
each grain of soil cries
Remember!
By bringing the soil back
at least here there is
a resting place
for someone close to us.
At the end of the war
the Germans
plowed all the buildings
to the ground.
Today Treblinka is a field
surrounded by trees and birds.
Last year
I separated the dirt
from the tiny flecks of bone
still in the dirt
but kept the urn
to hold these pieces of bone.

Who Held The Camera
So Steadily, And Why?

Photographs
at the Holocaust Museum:
In black and white
a naked girl,
maybe six,
gripped by the neck
in the hands of a woman
with huge biceps.
A mentally disturbed girl
shortly before her murder.
Near the dangling girl
is a photo in summer—

trees are fully leafed,
dark smoke pours
out of one building.
Down the hall
a young man with glasses
takes aim at a man
kneeling
in front of a pit of bodies;
the pistol points at the neck
so no shattered bone
will fly his way.

Warehouse
Of Twelve Million Tears

Washington Post:
A nondescript warehouse
sits in an industrial park
in Maryland suburbs,
unmarked, anonymous,
the only indication
that something unusual
resides there
is the way the front door
is locked whenever
anyone goes in or out.
Inside, a couple of offices,
a lab, a conference room,
gray space with row on row
of metal shelves, files,
plastic bins of what's left
from *Hitler's Final Solution:*
household goods
ripped from their owners
as bayonets slashed glass;

camp uniforms
torn and stained
a half century ago;
a wooden cart for
transporting bodies;
a narrow,
low-to-the-ground
dissecting table
with
a rim around its edges
to prevent a corpse from
rolling off—
a draining hole
the size of a quarter
for body fluids.
Down the hall,
boxes of human hair
from Auschwitz to Majdanek;
from the ground
beneath Lodz Ghetto.
Hundreds of pairs of shoes
found
at the killing centers
are being frozen
to destroy any bacteria
that could cause more
deterioration,
as fabric stars
and triangles
mould
like the farewell note
from a captured French
resistance fighter
to his family:
I'll probably be dead
by the time you get this.

In Storage For
The Holocaust Museum

Some objects in drawers
lined with acid-free paper,
others have form-fitting
styrofoam nests—
sometimes on top of
layers of protection
and support.
Nothing is touched directly.
White cotton gloves
are brought out
for the smallest task.
An instrument on a shelf
in the middle of the room
ticks away,
measuring fluctuations
in humidity and temperature.
Boxes of human hair.
Boxes labeled
victims belongings, slave labor.
Combs, toothbrushes, spoons,
scissors, graters, razors.
Faces with hairstyles and
clothes from the early Forties
peer from one box
filled with identity cards
and passports.
Civilian trousers
painted with a slapdash X
(a hasty substitute
for uniforms during times
when a camp ran out).
Cans that held Zyklon B
pellets for the gas chamber.

A pair of baby's pajamas
made from the mother's
night gown.
A table of enameled
feeding bowls—
many pierced with holes to
attach to the owner's clothes
(if you lost your bowl
you did not eat).
So many relics
exquisitely cared for,
unlike their original owners.
Last notes:
a shred of a shred with
Nothing that is happening
could be believed
written in three languages.
And in one corner,
a Danish rescue boat.

I Have Survived

And while enduring
the most atrocious torments,
still see my mother's
expression giving me
strength to survive.
At Auschwitz
someone told me
If you resist until
you leave this hell,
tell the world about us.
We want to remain
among the living—
at least on paper.

The Poems